D1064563

# What's Inside Me?
# My Lungs

## ¿Qué hay dentro de mí?
## Los pulmones

## Dana Meachen Rau

Marshall Cavendish
Benchmark
New York

# My Lungs

## Los pulmones

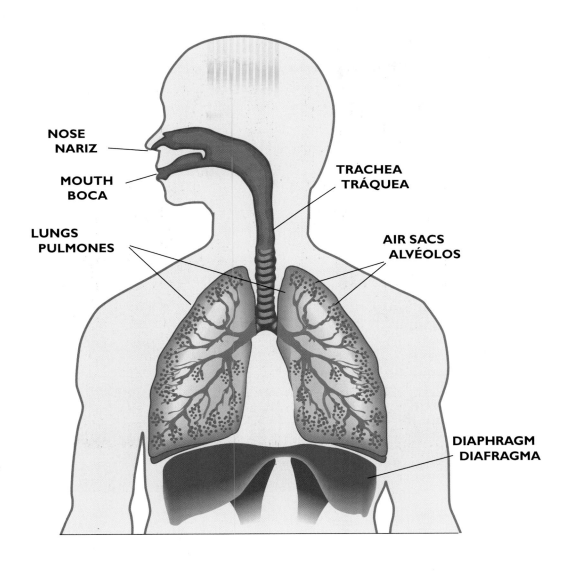

NOSE
NARIZ

MOUTH
BOCA

LUNGS
PULMONES

TRACHEA
TRÁQUEA

AIR SACS
ALVÉOLOS

DIAPHRAGM
DIAFRAGMA

3

4

Take a deep breath. Fresh air feels good on a summer day.

Air is all around you. It is filled with *oxygen*.

Respira profundamente. Da gusto respirar aire fresco en un día de verano.

El aire a tu alrededor está cargado de *oxígeno*.

You need oxygen to use your brain. You need it to move your arms and legs. Every part of your body needs oxygen to do its job.

Your body takes in oxygen by breathing. Your body breathes all the time.

Tu cerebro necesita oxígeno. Lo necesitas para mover los brazos y las piernas. Cada parte de tu cuerpo necesita oxígeno para trabajar.

Cuando respiras, el cuerpo toma oxígeno. Tu cuerpo respira todo el tiempo.

Air also has *carbon dioxide*. Your body makes carbon dioxide. When you breathe out, your body is getting rid of carbon dioxide.

El aire también tiene *dióxido de carbono*. Tu cuerpo produce dióxido de carbono, y cuando espiras, el cuerpo se libra de él.

You hold your breath when you swim underwater. You can stay underwater for only a short time. Your body needs air.

Cuando nadas debajo del agua, contienes la respiración. Puedes estar debajo del agua sólo por un rato. El cuerpo necesita aire.

Your lungs are like two spongy balloons inside your chest. They fill up with air every time you breathe in.

———————❖———————

Tus pulmones son como dos esponjas dentro del pecho que se llenan de aire cada vez que inspiras.

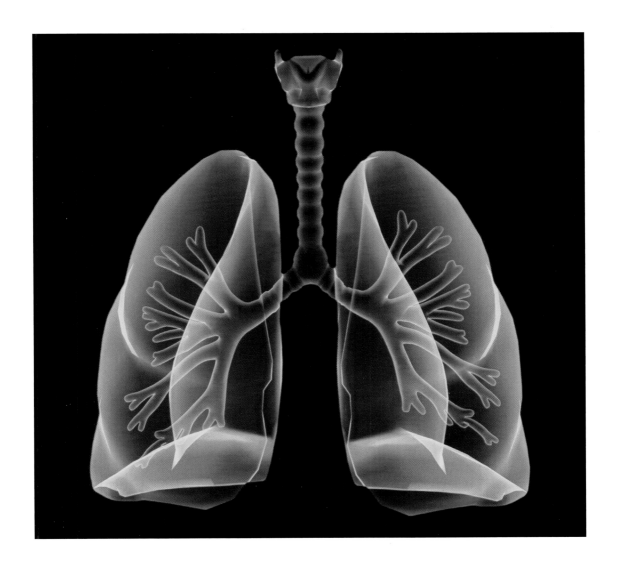

13

How does air get to your lungs? First it comes into your body through your mouth or nose.

You have hairs inside your nose. You also have *mucus*. These hairs and mucus trap dust so it will not go into your body.

¿Cómo entra el aire en los pulmones? Primero entra en tu cuerpo por la boca o la nariz.

Dentro de tu nariz hay vellos y mucosa. Los vellos y la *mucosa* atrapan el polvo para que no entre en tu cuerpo.

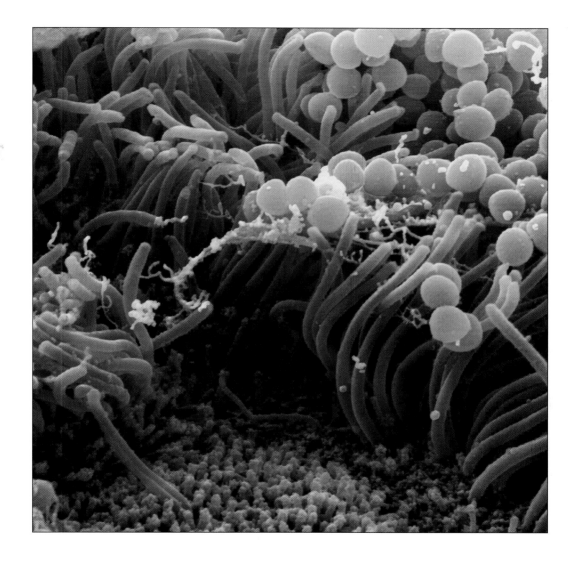

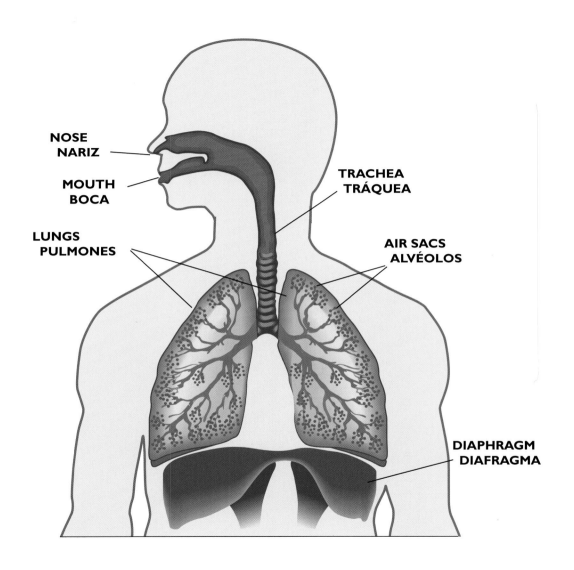

NOSE
NARIZ

MOUTH
BOCA

LUNGS
PULMONES

TRACHEA
TRÁQUEA

AIR SACS
ALVÉOLOS

DIAPHRAGM
DIAFRAGMA

Next the air travels down a tube called the *trachea*, or windpipe. Your trachea splits into two tubes. Each tube goes to a lung.

Inside your lungs, the tubes keep splitting. They look like branches on an upside-down tree.

Luego, el aire baja por un tubo llamado *tráquea* que se divide en dos. Cada tubo baja a un pulmón.

Dentro de los pulmones, los tubos se siguen dividiendo. Parecen las ramas de un árbol invertido.

There are groups of tiny *air sacs* at the end of each branch. The air sacs fill up with air. They look like bunches of tiny grapes.

There are more than 300 million air sacs in each of your lungs.

Al final de cada rama hay unos saquitos de aire llamados *alvéolos*. Los alvéolos se llenan de aire y parecen racimos de uvas diminutas.

Hay más de 300 millones de alvéolos en cada pulmón.

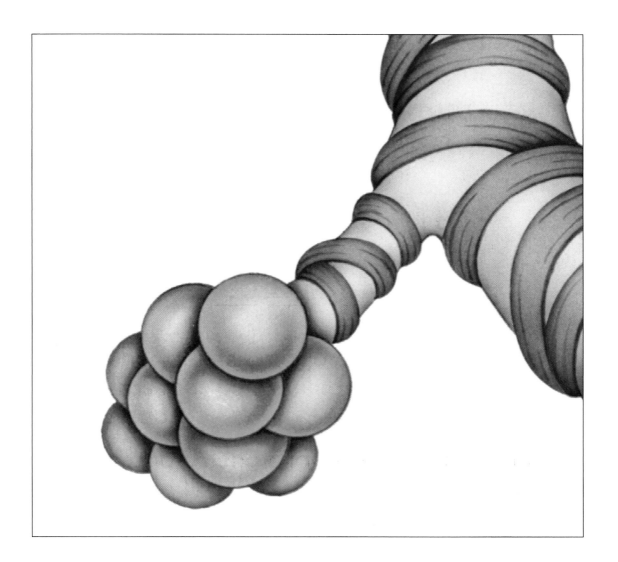

19

Oxygen moves from the air sacs into your blood. Your blood carries oxygen all around your body.

Carbon dioxide from your blood goes into the air sacs.

It travels back up the tubes and out of your mouth or nose when you breathe out.

El oxígeno va de los alvéolos a tu sangre, y la sangre lleva el oxígeno por todo el cuerpo.

El dióxido de carbono que está en la sangre entra en los alvéolos.

Sube por los tubos hacia la boca o la nariz y sale cuando espiras.

Your lungs get very large when you *inhale*. There is a muscle under your lungs called the *diaphragm*. It becomes flat to make room for the air in your lungs.

The diaphragm moves upward when you *exhale*. This helps push the air out of your lungs.

Tus pulmones se agrandan cuando *inhalas*. Hay un músculo debajo de tus pulmones llamado *diafragma* que se aplana para que el aire pueda entrar en los pulmones.

El diafragma se mueve hacia arriba cuando *exhalas* para sacar el aire de los pulmones.

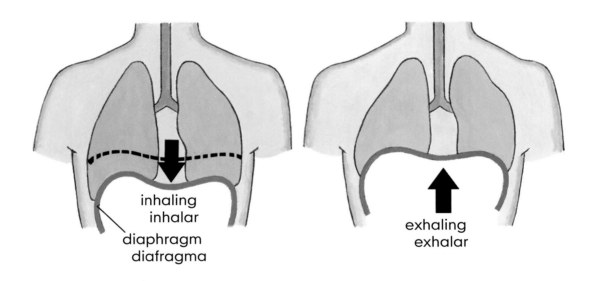

inhaling
inhalar

diaphragm
diafragma

exhaling
exhalar

23

24

Sometimes dust gets into your lungs. *Coughing* is the way your body gets dust out.

A cough is a burst of air that rushes from your lungs and out of your mouth.

A veces el polvo se mete en tus pulmones. *Toser* ayuda a que tu cuerpo saque el polvo. La tos es una salida brusca de aire por la boca, desde los pulmones.

*Sneezing* is another way your body gets rid of dust. Air from the lungs bursts out of your nose.

❖

*Estornudar* es otra manera en que tu cuerpo saca el polvo. El aire de tus pulmones sale de golpe por la nariz.

Every breath you take makes your body strong. Your lungs work hard to give your body the oxygen it needs to live.

Cada vez que respiras, tu cuerpo se fortalece. Tus pulmones están muy ocupados dándole a tu cuerpo el oxígeno que necesita para vivir.

## Challenge Words

**air sacs** Tiny balloons inside your lungs.

**carbon dioxide** The part of air your body does not need.

**coughing** A burst of air from your lungs out your mouth.

**diaphragm** A muscle under your lungs.

**exhale** To breathe out.

**inhale** To breathe in.

**mucus** A sticky material in your nose.

**oxygen** The part of air your body needs to work.

**sneezing** A burst of air from your lungs out your nose.

**trachea** The tube from your mouth to your lungs.

## Palabras avanzadas

**alvéolos** Unos saquitos de aire que están dentro de los pulmones.

**diafragma** Un músculo que está debajo de los pulmones.

**dióxido de carbono** La parte del aire que no necesita el cuerpo.

**estornudar** Es el aire de los pulmones que sale bruscamente por la nariz.

**exhalar** Espirar o soltar el aire.

**inhalar** Inspirar o dejar entrar el aire al cuerpo.

**mucosa** Una sustancia pegajosa que está dentro de la nariz.

**oxígeno** La parte del aire que el cuerpo necesita para trabajar.

**toser** Es el aire de los pulmones que sale bruscamente por la boca.

**tráquea** El tubo que va desde la boca hasta los pulmones.

# Index

# Índice

## With thanks to Nanci Vargus, Ed.D. and Beth Walker Gambro, reading consultants

Marshall Cavendish Benchmark
99 White Plains Road
Tarrytown, New York 10591-9001
www.marshallcavendish.us

Library of Congress Cataloging-in-Publication Data

Rau, Dana Meachen, 1971–
[My lungs. Spanish & English]
My lungs = Los pulmones / Dana Meachen Rau. — Bilingual ed.
p. cm. — (Bookworms. What's inside me? = ¿Qué hay dentro de mí?)
Includes index.
ISBN-13: 978-0-7614-2483-3 (bilingual edition)
ISBN-10: 0-7614-2483-0 (bilingual edition)
ISBN-13: 978-0-7614-2405-5 (Spanish edition)
ISBN-10: 0-7614-1780-X (English edition)
1. Respiratory organs—Juvenile literature. I. Title. II. Title: Los pulmones. III. Series:
Rau, Dana Meachen, 1971– Bookworms. What's inside me? (Spanish & English)

QP121.R3518 2006b
612.2—dc22
2006016713

Spanish Translation and Text Composition by Victory Productions, Inc.
www.victoryprd.com

Photo Research by Anne Burns Images

Cover photo by Corbis/Norbert Schaefer

The photographs in this book are used with the permission and through the courtesy of:
Corbis: pp. 1, 9, 20 Norbert Schaefer; p. 7 Jim Craigmyle; p. 10 Jim Cummins; p. 29 LWA-Dann Tardif.
Jay Mallin: p. 2. Visuals Unlimited: p. 4 Pegasus. Photo Researchers, Inc.: p. 13
Alfred Pasieka/Science PhotoLibrary; p. 15 Science Photo Library; p. 24 Carolyn A. McKeone;
p. 27 Damien Lovegrove/Science Photo Library. Custom Medical Stock Photo: pp. 19, 23.

Series design by Becky Terhune

Printed in Malaysia
1  3  5  6  4  2